EARNING, SAVING, SPENDING

Money

Margaret Hall

Heinemann Library
Chicago, Illinois

Customer Service 888-454-2279
Visit our website at www.heinemannlibrary.com

Designed by Kimberly R. Miracle and Cavedweller Studio
Photo research by Tracy Cummins and Heather Mauldin
Illustration by Mark Preston Illustration
Printed and bound in China by Leo Paper Products Ltd.

12
10 9 8 7 6 5 4

New edition ISBNS: 978-1-4034-9815-1 (hardcover)
                    978-1-4034-9820-5 (paperback)

Library of Congress Cataloging-in-Publication Data
Hall, Margaret, 1947-
  Money / Margaret Hall. -- 2nd ed.
     p. cm. -- (Earning, saving, spending)
  Includes bibliographical references and index.
  Summary: This text give students an overview of money providing details on
the evolution of currency, the making of coins and bills, and basics of use
around the world.
  ISBN 978-1-4034-9815-1 (hc) -- ISBN 978-1-4034-9820-5 (pb)
  1. Money--History--Juvenile literature. I. Title.
  HG231.H35 2008
  332.4--dc22
                                   2007015151

Acknowledgments
The author and publishers are grateful to the following for permission to reproduce copyright
material: Alamy **p. 7** (Rob Bartee); AP Photo **p.18** (J. Scott Applewhite); Mike Brosilow **pp.
11, 12, 19**; Corbis **pp. 6** (The Art Archive), **28** (William Whitehurst); Getty Images **pp. 5** (MPI),
8 (Royalty free), **14** (Royalty free), **15** (Royalty free), **20 all** (Royalty free), **22** (Colorblind Images
LLC), **25** (Donald Smetzer), **29** (Royalty free); Heinemann Raintree **pp. 9** (David Rigg), **17** (David
Rigg); Northwind Picture Archives **p. 4** (Nancy Carter); PhotoEdit **pp. 21** (David Young-Wolff),
24 (Michael Newman); Shutterstock **pp. 10** (Christy Thompson), **16** (J. Helgason), **23** (Danny E
Hooks); United States Mint **p. 13**.

Cover photographs reproduced with permission of Royalty free/Getty Images and Royalty free/
Getty Images (piggybank).

Every effort has been made to contact copyright holders of any material reproduced in this book.
Any omissions will be rectified in subsequent printings if notice is given to the publisher.

Disclaimer
All the Internet addresses (URLs) given in this book were valid at the time of going to press.
However, due to the dynamic nature of the Internet, some addresses may have changed, or sites
may have changed or ceased to exist since publication. While the author and publisher regret any
inconvenience this may cause readers, no responsibility for any such changes can be accepted by
either the author or the publisher.

Contents

Some words are shown in bold, **like this**. You can find out what they mean by looking in the glossary.

Before Money

A long time ago, there was no money. People did not need any. They grew, gathered, or hunted their food. They built their own houses and made their own clothing. Sometimes people had things that others wanted. A person who made beautiful pots might want a basket that another person made. So they would **barter**, or trade, with each other.

Native Americans traded with each other throughout North America, exchanging ideas and experiences as well as **goods**.

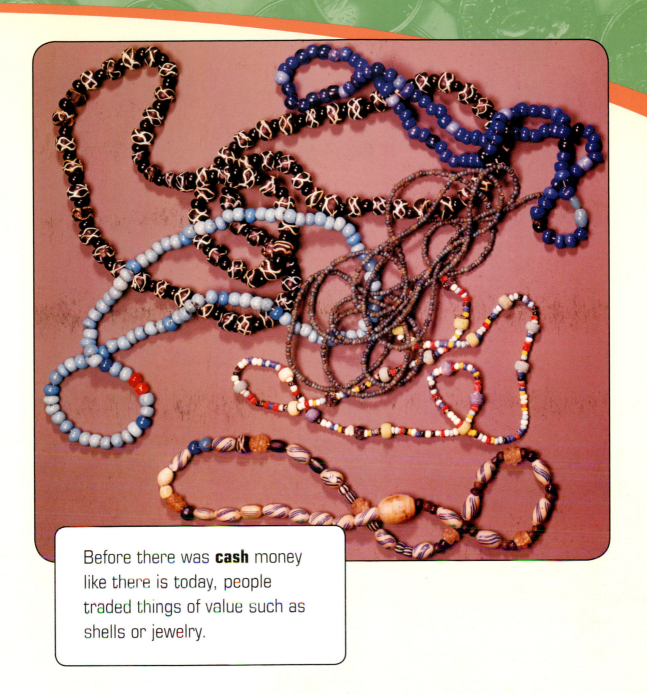

Before there was **cash** money like there is today, people traded things of value such as shells or jewelry.

Bartering worked most of the time. But sometimes people could not agree about what was fair. So they started to trade objects that had value to everyone. Salt, grains, feathers, tea leaves, shells, beads, and even fish hooks were used like money is used today.

The First Money

Before using money, the ancient Egyptians traded things like wheat and barley in exchange for metals, animals, spices, and lumber.

As time passed, people traveled farther from home to trade. It was hard to carry things like salt and shells. Someone came up with a better idea. Everyone agreed that metals like gold and silver were valuable. So people started to use them for trade. They made the metal into bars, lumps, or circles—the first **coins**.

Before long, people all over the world used coins to trade for things. Many coins they used did not look like the ones used today. But, like modern coins, they were easy to carry and had value.

Like today's coins, some coins used long ago had a picture of a **government** leader on them.

Money Today

Today, most people do not **barter** for the things they need. They use money instead. **Coins** are still used, but they are only one kind of money. Another is paper money, or **bills**.

Now, people use coins and bills to buy things they need or want.

The way money looks keeps changing. New coins and bills are made with different words and symbols on them. The materials used change, too. Instead of gold and silver, today's coins are made from combinations of more common metals, such as copper and nickel.

The United States **government** changes the look of some bills to make it difficult for people to make **illegal** money.

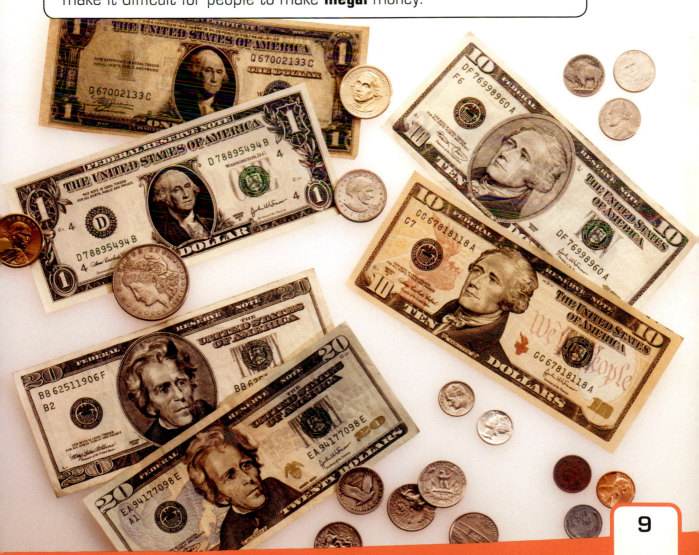

The Value of Money

Because money has value, people can exchange it for **goods** and **services**.

Coins and **bills** are not worth much by themselves. The metals and paper used to make them do not cost much. So why do people think money is valuable?

Money comes with a promise from the **government**. The promise is that every coin and bill is **legal tender**. That means that they can be used to pay for things. The government of the United States makes all the country's money. It is against the law for anyone else to make it. That is one reason why people trust the government's promise.

This is the government's promise.

Coins

There are six **coins** of different value used in the United States. How big a coin is does not tell you how much it is worth. Look at the dime. It is smaller than a penny or nickel, but it is worth more. Sometimes the U.S. **government** makes special coins.

Pennies, nickels, dimes, and quarters are the most common types of coin found in the United States.

Coins, such as these dollar coins, often show pictures of people who are important in American history.

The government made 50 different quarters to represent each of the 50 states. There are also special dollar coins to represent American presidents. Some coins are only made for a short amount of time. The Susan B. Anthony dollar coin is one of these. She was a famous American who worked to give women equal rights. People can still use the coins even though they are rare.

Making Coins

Coins come from a **mint**. A mint is a factory for making coins. A coin starts out as a thin strip of metal. One machine acts like a cookie cutter. It cuts the metal into circles called blanks.

These pennies and nickels all started as blank circles.

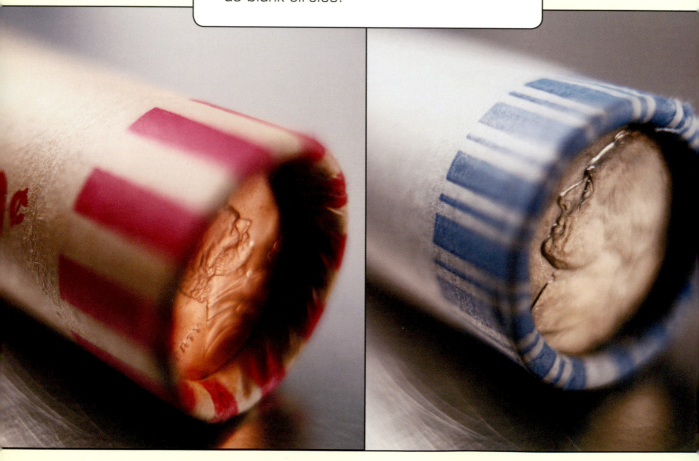

These letters tell where the coin was made.

"D" means the coin was made in Denver, Colorado.

"P" means the coin was made in Philadelphia, Pennsylvania.

The blanks travel to a machine that has special stamps called **dies**. The dies stamp symbols on both sides of the blanks. Coins are made very carefully. Every coin must look the same and weigh the same as other coins with that value.

Paper Money

There are different kinds of paper money, or **bills**. In the United States, they are all the same size, but each has different words and symbols printed on it. And each is worth a different amount of money.

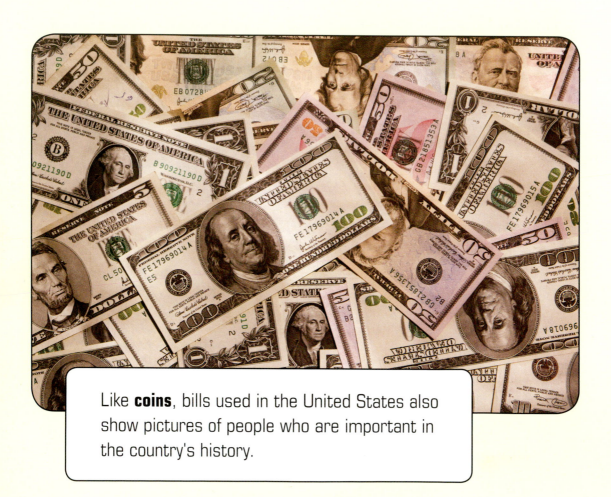

Like **coins**, bills used in the United States also show pictures of people who are important in the country's history.

Paper money does not weigh much or take up much space. So it is easier to carry than coins. A bill is usually worth more than a coin, too. If a book costs five dollars, it is easy to pay for it with a five-dollar bill. It would take 500 pennies to pay for the same book!

A five-dollar bill is equal to 500 pennies. Sometimes it is easier to carry bills than coins.

Making Paper Money

Paper money is made at the Bureau of Engraving and Printing, in Washington, D.C. Special paper and ink are used to make paper money. The paper starts out with nothing on it. Then it goes through a machine called a **printing press** that puts words and symbols on both sides.

Paper money is printed in large sheets and then cut to make each **bill**.

This is the serial number on a one-dollar bill.

Every one-dollar bill has many of the same words and symbols printed on it. But the bills are not exactly alike. Each one has its own special number, called a **serial number**. No other bill will have that number. The same thing is true for other kinds of bills.

Earning Money

People work to earn the money they need. The money they earn is their **income**. There are many ways to earn an income. Some people work in factories or restaurants. Some people deliver packages or mail. Others take care of sick people or teach in schools.

A person can use his or her education, special skills, or training to work to earn an income.

After working hard, it can feel good to receive a paycheck.

An **employer** pays a person money for the work he or she does. Many workers get their pay in the form of a **paycheck**. Some workers choose to let their employer put their pay directly into the worker's bank account. This is called **direct deposit**. If you get paid for doing things like chores at home or helping a neighbor, the money you earn is your income.

How Money Is Used

People use the money they earn in many ways. People spend some of their **income** on **goods** and **services**. Goods are things people use, like clothing, houses—even toys. Services are things that are done for someone else. People pay doctors, teachers, waiters, and others for the services those workers provide.

People must spend their money wisely, so they have enough to buy the things they really need.

The more money a person earns, the more taxes he or she must pay.

Most people save part of their income so they will have money in the future. And many people give some money away to help others. People must also pay **taxes**. The **government** uses tax money to pay government workers and to build things, such as roads and schools.

Making Choices About Money

People must use at least part of their income to buy things they need, like food.

There are many ways to spend money. Most people use much of their **income** to pay for their needs. These are things they must have. Food to eat, clothing to wear, and a place to live are all needs.

People also spend money on wants. Wants are things they would like to have, but could do without. Televisions, toys, and fancy cars are all wants. How to spend is not the only choice people make about money. They also decide how much to save and how much to give away. If they use their money wisely, they can do some of each.

Many people set aside part of their income to buy things for fun.

Where Money Goes

When someone spends money, where does it go? Money travels from person to person and place to place. The five-dollar **bill** used to buy a book today might be in another town by next week. Just follow the travels of this bill.

1 A man gives a store clerk in Chicago, Illinois, a five-dollar bill to pay for a book.

2 The clerk gives the same bill to a woman as change.

3 The woman puts the same bill in a birthday card for her nephew.

Money does not last forever. **Coins** get scratched or bent. Paper money gets dirty or ripped. But money is not thrown away when it gets old. The old money is sent back to the **government**. Coins are melted down at the **mint** and the metal is used again. Old bills are burned, or shredded and recycled.

4 The mail carrier in Chicago picks up the card so it can be delivered.

5 The nephew in Dallas, Texas, takes the card from the mailbox.

6 He buys a toy and pays for it with the same five-dollar bill.

Money Around the World

The money used in other countries does not look like the money used in the United States. That is because almost every country makes its own money, or **currency**.

Bills from different countries do not look the same.

Each currency is different. **Coins** and **bills** from different places have different values and usually have different names. The symbols and words that appear on them are not the same either.

People can exchange one currency for another at a bank or currency exchange.

Some money can be used in more than one country. The euro is one kind that can be used in many different countries in Europe. When people visit countries other than their own, they usually have to use that country's currency. They can exchange one currency for the other. Understanding money is important almost everywhere in the world.

Glossary

barter to trade one thing for another without using money

bill paper money

cash coins and paper money

coin flat piece of metal used as money

currency money used in a certain country or continent

die tool used to stamp numbers and symbols on coins

direct deposit way of paying a worker by putting money right into his or her bank account

employer person or business for whom other people work for pay

goods things people buy, such as food, clothing, and toys

government leadership of a country, state, or town

illegal against the law

income money a person receives from jobs and other sources

legal tender money that the government says can be used to pay for things

mint factory where coins are made

paycheck money a person earns for work he or she has done

printing press machine that puts words and symbols on paper

serial number special number used to identify an item

service something done for someone

tax money paid to the government for public services

Find Out More

Cribb, Joe. *Money.* New York: DK Children, 2005.

Rau, Dana Meachen. *The History of Money.*
    Milwaukee, WI: Gareth Stevens, 2006.

Samuel, Charlie. *Money and Finance in Colonial
    America.* New York: PowerKids Press, 2003.

To learn more about money in the United States, visit the
United States Department of the Treasury Education website
at: http:/www.ustreas.gov/education/

Index